Affirmations
for
A Woman
of
Worth

1 Hope You Dance!

Dr. Jacquelyn Hadnot

Contents

Affirmations for A Woman of Worth: I Hope You Dance!

Dedication
I Hope You Dance

What started out as a chapter in the first installment in the Woman of Worth series *Loving the Skin I'm In*, *"How Can I Dance if You are Standing on My Feet"* has now evolved into a life "book" of its own. I never thought God would use me to write a book of affirmations that would empower women. I have written many books, but for me this is the first book of its kind.

I count it a privilege and an honor to birth this empowerment message to the women of God. *"Affirmations for a Woman of Worth: I Hope You Dance"* is encouragement and empowerment at its best. Why? Because it speaks to women from every walk of life who share the same challenges, struggles, fears and tears. For every woman who has traveled the Woman of Worth journey with me, you will understand why the message in this book is so vital to our growth.

To help you understand why this book is important I am including excerpts from *Loving the Skin I'm In*. I pray it will help you to get a deeper understanding of what it means to dance.

It is my prayer that this book moves you to another place in your confidence, joy, peace, healing, freedom, and overall prosperity: mentally, physically, emotionally and financially. The Lord desires our prosperity in every area and our situations will not change until we change. It is time for change and change begins with the way in which we speak. The words that proceed from our mouths have power. Positive or negative, productive or destructive - our words carry power. We must begin to walk in the power and authority that has been given to us by Christ Jesus, but we cannot walk in that power until we harness the power of our tongue because life and death are in the power of the tongue. What are you chewing on? Are you still chewing on past hurts and pains? Is every bitter bite keeping you in bondage to your past? It is time to change your diet and begin eating from the good of the land and all that the Lord has for you. It is time to access the authority given to you by the Lord, walk in His power, taking authority over the often-venomous tongue that has kept you bound and down for too long.

It is time that you learn or relearn how to dance. It is time that you throw the past hurts, pains and shames off your feet and dance. It is time that you put the player haters, instigators, agitators, and naysayer's off the dance floor of your life and if necessary dance the dance of victory just you and the Father. Stand on your Heavenly Father's feet and dance. As you twirl around the floor, allow every weight and snare to fall off. I hope you dance as the rays of the SON shine on your face. I hope you giggle like schoolgirl on her first date as you dance with the Father. I hope the joy in your heart and the smile on your face light up an entire city block. My sisters, I hope you DANCE!

Affirmations for A Woman of Worth

I Hope You Dance!

Igniting the Fire Publishing

Affirmations for A Woman of Worth: I Hope You Dance!

What is an Affirmation?

An affirmation is the act of affirming or the state of being affirmed. It is something that is declared true, a positive statement or judgment. An affirmation is a simple statement, but it can change your life forever. Affirmations have the ability to move you from the mundane and mediocre. From the powerless to the powerful. From the minuscule to the magnificent. Affirmations are short statements, but they carry a level of power that can revolutionize your life. Never underestimate the power of the spoken word.

We have been told to watch the words that we speak because there is power in the tongue. It is true and the words that we speak have the ability to shape the fabric of our lives. The shape can be good or bad, positive or negative, constructive or destructive.

Just as there are positive words that flow from our lives, there are also negative words that will stop the flow in our lives. Negative words or word curses have been around since the beginning of time and have a way of following us down through the generations. That is why it is vital that we guard the words we speak.

According to research done on the subject, we have between 45,000 and 51,000 thoughts a day. The research also showed that the thoughts of some people are mostly negative and the percentage can go as high as 80%. If the average person is walking around thinking negative thoughts 80% of the time, it's no wonder our society is inundated with negative people.

The sad part is that these people may not recognize that they are walking poster children for "stinking thinking" and that their thinking is adversely influencing others around them.

Instead of telling a child that he is dumb, why not remind the child that he or she is smart and can accomplish anything they set their mind to achieve.

Instead of telling a family member who is on drugs that he is good for nothing, why not affirm that one day the addiction will be a thing of the past and he will walk in the fullness and wholeness of life. We must begin to make positive declarations or affirmations over our lives and the lives of everyone we care for.

Ladies, it is time to speak life. It is time that we walk in the power and authority given to us by Christ Jesus. It is time that we raise the bar when it comes to what we think, how we speak and what we are willing to accept. As we begin the process of renewing our minds, we must ask questions that are vital to the change that we must embrace. We cannot continue to allow the negative Nancy's to infiltrate our thought processes with destructive language. We are Kingdom women and as Kingdom women, we won't settle for less than God's best. It also means that we won't settle for the garbage of others and we won't allow ourselves to be garbage disposals for their problems, negative attitudes or drama-ridden lives. Nothing will hinder your ability to dance than having individuals use you as a dumping ground for their seemingly endless parade of drama, confusion and problems.

You must consider several things when engaging in conversations that could ultimately drag you into a web of lies, deceit, confusion and DRAMA.

- ✓ What is the INTENTION of the person through the information they are conveying? Are they conveying information that will encourage or inspire? Or are they dropping gossip and drama into your lap?

- ✓ Have they ASSOCIATED you with problem solving, backbiting or gossiping?

✓ Will the conversation bring SOLUTIONS or DISTRACTIONS? There is nothing worse than being caught in a web of distractions.

When you ask yourself these three questions honestly and openly, if will help determine what level of conversation is needed when dealing with individuals.

What are affirmations? They are positive statements that can change your life. They can literally revolutionize the way you view any situation. Affirmations are stepping-stones to fulfilling your destiny. With affirmations, you will move your life from mundane and mediocre to magnificent and marvelous. When you understand how to apply affirmations to your mindset, you will possess a powerful tool for achieving success, improving and transforming your life.

Today is the day that you begin to speak life into every situation, circumstance and life that you encounter. You are a woman of worth and it is time to get started speaking life into your womb of destiny.

How to Use this Book of Empowering Affirmations

"Be transformed by the renewing of your mind."

Your thoughts become words and your words become actions.

Your words and thoughts program the mind in the same way that commands and scripts program a computer. By using this process consciously and intently, you influence your subconscious mind, and in turn, it transforms your habits, behavior, attitude, and reactions, and even reshapes your external life.[1]

As with any resource material, there are essential steps to follow in order to maximize your success and achieve the lasting effects you desire. I suggest the following six steps in order to get the most out of the affirmations in this book. Remember, your thoughts become words and your words become actions. So a woman thinks, so she is…

How to use this book:

1. Pray and ask the Lord to reveal the affirmations that apply to your life.

2. Read through the entire book and identify the affirmations you want to focus on. It might be helpful to focus on one category at a time.

3. Write out the affirmations in a journal and review them regularly.

4. Stand in front of a mirror and speak the affirmations out loud each morning and every night before you go to bed. As you repeat the affirmations, begin to see what you desire as established in your life.

5. Once or twice a day, sit down and write out each of the affirmations at least 10 times. This is your way of solidifying it in your spirit.

6. You need a dream board. A dream board brings your affirmations to the forefront. Create small posters using a program such as Microsoft Word or PowerPoint. Use one page per affirmation and type it in large letters. Post it where you can see it and read it several times per day.

Make affirmations a lifestyle:

1. Choose affirmations that pertain to the areas you are dealing with.

2. Repeat your affirmations every chance you get. You should also repeat them in quiet moments several times a day.

3. Relax as you recite your affirmations.

4. Pay attention to the words you are speaking.

5. The stronger your faith in what you are speaking, the greater your results.

6. Choose positive words avoiding any negative statements that will hinder your growth.

7. When making statements of affirmation, always speak of your situation in the present tense.

8. We should never be shaken by the things that we see. Therefore, don't allow your current situation to hinder the words that you speak about your future. See your future as already accomplished in the earth realm.

It's Time to Speak those things...

How Can I Dance When You're Standing on My Feet?

Excerpts from A Woman of Worth: Loving the Skin I'm In

I love to dance because dancing is a form of praise, release, freedom and in some instances flight. Do you remember when you were a child and you danced on the feet of your earthly father? You held on tight as he danced you around the room. With a giggle and wide-eyed smile, it almost felt like flying. There was freedom in the dance as you twirled around the room. As you grew into a teenager and went to parties and other affairs, if you were like me, you would dance, with or without a partner because dancing was your outlet.

Fast forward to the place you are now and ask yourself, *"Do I still enjoy dancing?"* My husband and I will dance around the family room to whatever music is playing because it is a form of togetherness and it brings us joy and laughter. Whether I am dancing with Gregg or alone - I love to dance.

During my season of going through the valley of devaluation, I found myself asking the question, how can I dance if you are standing on my feet? How can you dance with the freedom of an eagle if someone is standing on your feet? Unlike, the little girl who stood on her father's feet and danced, you are incapable of moving in the spirit when your spiritual feet are in bondage, weighed down with the cares of the world.

When Satan is standing on your feet, how can you dance? When fear, doubt or insecurity sits on your heart like a ton of bricks, how can you dance? When the world has placed a low jack on your self-worth, how can you dance? When everyone around you tells you that you will never amount to anything, how can you dance? When the people in your inner circle turn their backs on you, and scandalize your name, how can you dance? When the people you placed in leadership positions in the church lie, connive and split the church, how can you dance? When the husband you love, trusted and believed in devalues the marriage and blames you for it, how can you dance?

Well, my dear sister when any scenario happens, dancing just might be the only thing you have left. It may sound strange, but the enemy has designed your downfall by trying to take away your ability to dance. He wants you to retreat into a little corner and cower like a weak, pitiful little girl with no power or authority. He wants you to kick off your dancing shoes, throw them in the trash and stomp off defeated, bruised and rejected. Moreover, there may be days when that's how you feel, but that's not who you are. There may also be days, when you just don't feel like being anything, except left alone.

As a woman who has been in that dark lonely place, I can tell you that it's because you just don't have the strength to dance. The day I almost lost my strength to dance was the day that the enemy THOUGHT I was defeated. OH! The devil is a liar. Yes, I was down and retreated for a season. Yes, I thought my days of writing and birthing music were over and yes, I thought about getting a job and leaving ministry behind. BUT GOD! You can hide from many things and many people, but you cannot hide from God. It doesn't matter who is trying to kill your destiny, it is IMPOSSIBLE for them to kill something they did not give you in the first place. No man or woman on the face of the earth can stop your destiny because it is not in his or her weak manipulative power to accomplish such a great feat. They may hinder you for a while, they may even convince you to walk away for a season, but the destiny inside of you will not allow it, because greater is He that is in you than he that is in the world. Destiny and greatness are waiting to be birthed out of your spiritual belly.

Sometimes the "he" that is in the world might be your mother, father, sister, brother, husband or best friend. Watch out for the "he" that is trying to kill your seed by assassinating your ministry, character, destiny or self-worth.

Spiritual assassins are ready to shoot your legs right out from under you. Yes, I said spiritual assassins who might be sitting in the cubicle next to you. Whispering in your ear during lunch, shopping with you, spending your money and trying to cut off your spiritual legs at the same time. Spiritual assassins will try to cut the baby right out of your belly, leaving you empty and bloody. You must recognize what is operating against you. The "what" is not a flesh and blood enemy, it is Satan and his diabolical hosts from hell. They are assigned to steal, kill and destroy you. If Satan can kill your joy, he can steal your peace. If he can steal your peace, he can destroy your faith. If he can destroy your faith, you are dead to the plans and purposes of God. (Read Second Corinthians 10:4-5, Ephesians 6:10-18).

As a woman of worth and spiritual warrior, you must recognize the spies trying to infiltrate the camp. You must pull down every stronghold and imagination that tries to exalt itself against what you know to be true about your God and your destiny.

If you haven't danced in a while, put on some praise music and dance. Simply, dance. If you enjoy walking, cut a little strut while you are walking. STAND on the feet of your Heavenly Father and dance my dear sister, DANCE!

Affirmations for A Woman of Worth: I Hope You Dance!

Can You Stand the Rain?
The Rain Dance of an Overcomer

"The storms of life are not there to destroy you, allow them to strengthen you."

Let's face it; storms are a part of life. Good or bad, young or old, rich or poor—storms are no respecter of persons. It rains on the just and the unjust. The one deciding factor through it all is how you go through the storm. You have two choices, you can go through the storm murmuring and complaining or you can go through the storm learning life's lessons that will help you weather future storms. Complaining only makes your storm worse. Imagine being in the midst of your own personal tsunami with no way out and the only thing you can think of is giving up. Every depressing thought that you have ever had will come to mind when you are in the storm.

The distracting thoughts will also arise when you are in the midst of your most devastating storm. Fear, doubt, negativity, unbelief and the like will throw themselves at you when you are in the midst of a storm. The enemy wants to stop you from dancing, singing, smiling and even living. The result, life becomes a burden with no hope in sight. Remember, life is not about waiting for the storm to pass, it is about learning to dance in the midst of the storm. If you can dance your way through the storm, the storm won't seem so horrendous because your focus will not be on the storm. Your focus will be on how you got THROUGH THE STORM.

When the Disciples were in the boat, their focus was not on Jesus, their focus was on the storm. When you take your eyes off the Lord, the storm will seem like the most destructive thing you have ever encountered. Try keeping your eyes on the One who can calm every storm in your life. TRY JESUS!

Your ability to overcome the storm is directly related to your ability to keep your focus on the Storm Calmer as He speaks to the torrential storms in your life. When He says, *"Peace, be still"* and the winds of your storm obey His every command, that is the day that you know your storm is over and the promised rainbow of His presence is about to appear before your eyes.

You can begin the rain dance of an overcomer because the stormy days are over, the clouds are passing you by and the SON shine is about to shine in and through your life. You stood the rain, passed the test and His light is now shining on your ways. Know that the Lord has given you perfect peace from the battle that was raging against you. It is time to celebrate and dance the rain dance of an overcomer. Kick your shoes off, pull your hair back, and put on your celebratory music and DANCE! Dance with a reckless abandon that cries, *"I don't have a care in the world because the SON shine is shining brilliantly in my life. I am an overcomer and this is my dance of victory!"* This is the dance and testimony of an overcomer. My sisters, I sincerely hope you dance.

"*I AM*"
Affirmations for
A Woman of
Worth
Part 1

❏ I am a woman of worth and I have strength for all things in Christ who empowers me.

❏ I am ready for anything and equal to anything through Him Who infuses inner strength into me; I am self-sufficient in Christ's sufficiency.

❏ I am a woman of worth and it is God who arms me with strength and makes my way perfect. He armed me with strength for the battle and made my enemies bow at my feet.

❏ I am a woman of worth and the LORD is my strength and my shield; my heart trusts in him, and I am helped. My heart leaps for joy and I will give thanks to him in song.

❏ I am a woman of worth and God is my refuge and strength, an ever-present help when I am in trouble.

❏ I am a woman of worth and my flesh and my heart may fail, but God is the Rock and firm Strength of my heart and my Portion forever.

❏ I am a woman of worth and I will love the Lord my God out of and with my whole heart and out of and with all my soul, my life and out of and with all my mind, with my faculty of thought and my moral understanding and out of and with all my strength.

☐ I am a woman of worth and I thank Christ Jesus our Lord, who has given me strength, that He considered me faithful, appointing me to His service.

☐ I am a woman of worth and God's peace is mine, that tranquil state of a soul assured of its salvation through Christ, and so fearing nothing from God and being content with my earthly destiny, that peace which transcends all understanding shall guard over my heart and mind in Christ Jesus.

☐ I am a woman of worth and I will let the peace and harmony, which comes from Christ rule in my heart, deciding and settling with finality all questions that arise in my mind, in that peaceful state to which as a member of Christ's one body I am called to live. I will be thankful, giving praise to God always.

☐ I am a woman of worth and God's favor is on me today.

☐ I am a woman of worth and I expect God's

blessings in my life today.

- ☐ I am a woman of worth and God's mercy is on me today.

- ☐ I am a woman of worth and I will not die, but live and declare the works of the Lord.

- ☐ I am a woman of worth and I believe God has given me an abundant life.

- ☐ I am a woman of worth and goodness and mercy follow me wherever I go.

- ☐ I am a woman of worth and the battle is already won because the battle belongs to the Lord.

- ☐ I am a woman of worth and my God will do exceedingly, abundantly above all that I ask or think according to the power of God that works in me.

- ☐ I am a woman of worth and I am the head and not the tail. I am above and not beneath. I am blessed going in and blessed coming out.

- ☐ I am a woman of worth and God is preparing me for what He has ordained for me.

- ❏ I am a woman of worth and God's divine power has given me everything I need for life and godliness through my knowledge of him who called me by His own glory and goodness.

- ❏ I am a woman of great worth to God and myself.

- ❏ I AM the greatest untapped resource to mankind.

- ❏ I AM a woman who brings hope to the hopeless.

- ❏ I AM determined to give my best in everything.

- ❏ I AM among *the called* by God.

- ❏ I AM encouraged, inspired and motivated.

- ❏ I AM a seeker of wisdom and knowledge.

- ❏ I AM a woman who knows how to laugh.

- ❏ I AM **B**eautiful, **A**mazing and **D**estined for greatness. I AM BAD.

I am a woman of worth. I am beautiful, priceless & loved by God.

Affirmations of
an
Eagle
Part 2

The beauty of an eagle.

☐ I AM AN EAGLE BECAUSE: I soar above my situation and every trial looks small when I see it from God's perspective.

☐ I AM AN EAGLE BECAUSE: I do not hang around pigeons, chickens and buzzards. God uses me to minister to them in order to help them come out of the pigeon, chicken or buzzard mentality.

☐ I AM AN EAGLE BECAUSE: I do not eat on the dead things of my past and I do not chew on dead relationships, past hurts or pains.

☐ I AM AN EAGLE BECAUSE: My spiritual eyesight is keen and I can see the enemy's traps and snares and pray and press my way through them.

☐ I AM AN EAGLE BECAUSE: I am fearless in the face of the enemy's traps, snares and manipulations. I will never surrender to the size and strength of the enemy because my God is greater.

☐ I AM AN EAGLE BECAUSE: I am tenacious. When the storms rage pigeons, chickens and buzzards fly or run away, but I stretch out my wings of prayer and soar to greater heights in the Lord.

☐ I AM AN EAGLE BECAUSE: I am full of life, vision and wisdom. Like an eagle, when it is time to rest and reenergize, I retreat to the Secret Place of the Most High and allow Him to renew my strength. Also, like an eagle while I am in the Secret Place, the Lord takes me through a metamorphosis and I am rejuvenated physically, emotionally and spiritually to continue to run the Kingdom race.

❒ I AM AN EAGLE BECAUSE: No matter what tries to hinder my journey: storms, trials, adversities - STILL I RISE!

❒ I AM AN EAGLE and I live Isaiah 40:31. When I wait on the Lord, He renews my strength. I am able to mount up on strong, mighty wings, I can run the Kingdom race and not grow weary, and I can walk and not faint in the times of adversity.

❒ I am an eagle and everyday I rise! I am a woman of worth and today the Lord is calling me to arise and soar like the eagle I was created to be. ARISE EAGLE OF GOD, ARISE!

It does not matter what the day brings I will:

- ✓ Get out of bed.
- ✓ Throw my shoulders back.
- ✓ Shake the dust of sadness off my feet.
- ✓ Wash my face (no more tearstains).
- ✓ Take off my grave clothes.
- ✓ Put on the whole armor of God.
- ✓ Fix my weave.
- ✓ Put on my makeup.
- ✓ Stand in the mirror and proclaim.

  - ✶ They thought I was down.
  - ✶ The devil thought he had me bound.
  - ✶ My fre-nemies counted my out.
  - ✶ My family discounted me.

In spite of it all…

I AM AN EAGLE today and everyday I will RISE!

My outward beauty is an expression of my inward beauty and peace.

BEAUTY

My beauty should not come from outward adornment, such as braided hair and the wearing of gold jewelry and fine clothes.

1 Peter 3:3

…and provide for those who grieve in Zion—to bestow on them a crown of beauty instead of ashes.

Isaiah 61:3

Affirmations
From the
Fruit of the
Spirit
Part 3

Love

But the fruit of the Spirit is love, joy, peace, patience, kindness, goodness, faithfulness, gentleness and self-control.
        Galatians 5:22-23

I will walk in the Fruit of the Spirit of the Lord so that others will see His love through me.

Joy

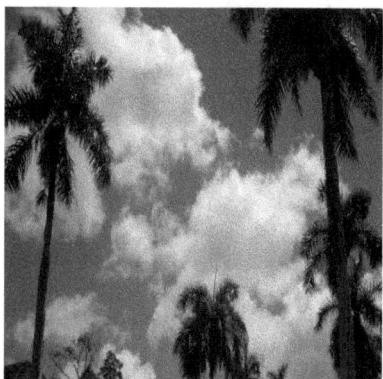

You have filled my heart with greater joy ...

Psalm 4:7

I take refuge in you and I am glad; I will forever sing for joy.

Kindness

...and to godliness, brotherly kindness; and to brotherly kindness, love.
2 Peter 1:7

I am God's chosen vessel, holy and dearly loved, clothed with compassion, kindness, humility, gentleness and patience.

Goodness

For this
very
reason,
make every effort to
add to your faith
goodness; and to
goodness,
knowledge.

2 Peter 1:5

Surely, goodness and love will follow me all the days of my life, and I will dwell in the house of the LORD forever.

Psalm 23:6

Self-Control

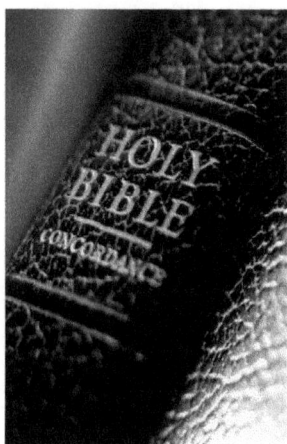

...and to knowledge, self-control; and to self-control, perseverance; and to perseverance, godliness.

2 Peter 1:6

Lord, grant me self-control in every area of my life, that I may please You.

Gentleness

Let your gentleness be evident to all.

Philippians 4:5

I am a woman of worth and my gentleness be evident to everyone I meet.

PEACE

I will lie down and sleep in peace, for you alone, O LORD, make me dwell in safety.

Psalm 4:8

When I will lie down, I sleep in peace, for you alone, O LORD, make me reside in safety and confident trust.

Faithfulness

O LORD, hear my prayer, listen to my cry for mercy; in your faithfulness and righteousness come to my relief.

Psalm 143:1

O LORD, hear your daughters prayer, listen to my cry for mercy; in your faithfulness and righteousness come to my relief.

Patience

...in purity, understanding, patience and kindness; in the Holy Spirit and in sincere love.

2 *Corinthians* 6:6

I am strengthened with all power according to His glorious might so that I may have great endurance and patience, and joyfully giving thanks to the Father, who has qualified me to share in the inheritance of the saints in the kingdom of light.
Colossians 1:11-12

Affirmations for a Woman with

Purpose & Destiny

Part 4

❏ I am determined with the power of God to walk in my dreams.

❏ I know that my potential lies in my ability to believe in my dreams.

❏ As long as I walk in the power of God, my potential is limitless.

❏ When I begin to walk out my dreams, God will provide the provisions for my vision.

❏ If no one else believes in my dreams, I believe.

❏ I will seek out other dreamers so that I will be inspired to press forward.

❏ I will align myself with other dreamers who share similar visions.

❏ God has given me dreams that must be fulfilled on the earth.

❏ My dreams have become the compass by which I set my sights on tomorrow.

☐ I realize that my dreams might be misunderstood in the eyes of man, but they are embraced by the heart of God.

☐ The dreams inside my womb will be a blessing to the world.

☐ I am walking in the destiny that God has for me.

☐ I will align myself with a support team that embraces the dream God has given me.

☐ My dream will bring glory to God.

☐ I embrace my God-given potential.

☐ My dream has become the Habakkuk 2:2 mandate for my life.

☐ Even when my dream is fulfilled, I will continue to dream until the day I die.

☐ I am forever a dreamer.

☐ I possess the power of God to get wealth based on Deuteronomy 8:18..

Dreams

" 'In the last days, God says, I will pour out my Spirit on all people. Your sons and daughters will prophesy, your young men will see visions, your old men will dream dreams."

Acts 2:17

There is a dream inside my belly that I will fulfill.

DESTINY

"For I know the plans I have for you," declares the LORD, "plans to prosper you and not to harm you, plans to give you hope and a future."
Jeremiah 29:11

There is a destiny for me and I will walk according to the divine plan that is designed to give me hope and a future.

Hope

"So there is hope for your future," declares the LORD.
Jeremiah 31:17

God knows the plans He has for me, plans to prosper me and not to harm me, plans to give me hope and a future.

Influence

By the blessing of the influence of the upright and God's favor [because of them] the city is exalted.

Proverbs 11:11

By the blessing of the influence of the upright and God's favor because of us our city is exalted.

Inheritance

Ask of me, and I will make the nations your inheritance, the ends of the earth your possession.

Psalm 2:8

The boundary lines of the Lord have fallen for me in pleasant places; surely, I have a delightful inheritance.

Psalm 16:6

POWER

May the God of hope fill you with all joy and peace as you trust in him, so that you may overflow with hope by the power of the Holy Spirit.

Romans 15:13

I am a woman of worth and the God of hope has filled me with all joy and peace as I trust in him, so that I may overflow with hope by the power of the Holy Spirit.

Prosperity

He will spend his days in prosperity, and his descendants will inherit the land.

Psalm 25:13

I will spend my days in prosperity, and my descendants will inherit the land.

Purpose

But I have raised you up for this very purpose, that I might show you my power and that my name might be proclaimed in all the earth.

Exodus 9:16

God Has raised me up for this very purpose, that He might show His power through my life and that His name might be proclaimed in all the earth.

Vision

And the LORD answered me, and said, Write the vision, and make it plain upon tables, that he may run that readeth it. For the vision is yet for an appointed time, but at the end it shall speak, and not lie: though it tarry, wait for it; because it will surely come, it will not tarry.

Habakkuk 2:2-3

I will write the vision, and make it plain upon tables, so that as I read it I can run with it. For the vision is yet for an appointed time, but at the end it shall speak, and not lie: though it tarry, I will wait for it; because it will surely come, it will not tarry.

Affirmations
for an
Overcomer

Part 5

❏ Guide me in your truth and teach me, for you are God my Savior, and my hope is in You all day long. Psalms 25:5

❏ May integrity and uprightness protect me, because my hope is in you. Psalms 25:21

❏ I wait in hope for the LORD; he is my help and my shield. Psalms 33:20

❏ In him, my hearts rejoice, for I trust in his holy name. Psalms 33:21

❏ May Your unfailing love rest upon me, O LORD, even as I put our hope in you. Psalms 33:22

❏ In His name I will put my hope." Mt 12:21

❏ I am joyful in hope, patient in affliction, and faithful in prayer. Romans 12:12

❏ My hope is in You and no one whose hope is in You will ever be put to shame. Psalm 25:3

❏ I am an overcomer by the blood of the Lamb, and by the word of my testimony. Revelation 12:11

☐ I will dance and be glad the Lord will turn my mourning into gladness; He will give me comfort and joy instead of sorrow. Jeremiah 31:13

☐ Weeping may endure for a night, but joy will come when I awake in the morning.

☐ I will trust in the Lord with all my heart and I will not lean on my own understanding of things, but in all my ways I will acknowledge the Lord and allow Him to direct my paths (Proverbs 3:3-5).

HOPE

No one whose hope is in you will ever be put to shame, but they will be put to shame who are treacherous without excuse.

Psalm 25:3

My hope
is in the
Lord who
sustains
me.

Overcomer

And they overcame him by the blood of the Lamb, and by the word of their testimony.

Revelation 12:11

I AM AN OVERCOMER OF EVERY CHALLENGE AND OBSTACLE THAT COMES INTO MY LIFE.

DANCE

A time to weep and a time to laugh, a time to mourn and a time to dance.
Ecclesiastes 3:4

I will dance and be glad the Lord will turn my mourning into gladness; He will give me comfort and joy instead of sorrow.

Jeremiah 31:13

Goodness

How can I repay the LORD for all his goodness to me?

Psalm 116:12

The fruit of the light I walk in consists in all goodness, righteousness and truth.

Peace

...to shine on those living in darkness and in the shadow of death, to guide our feet into the path of peace."

Luke 1:79

Lord,
guide my
feet into
the path
of peace.

Tests

Then the LORD said to Moses, "I will rain down bread from heaven for you. The people are to go out each day and gather enough for that day. In this way, I will test them and see whether they will follow my instructions.

Exodus 16:4

Tests, trials and travail I have tasted them all, but now I am eating from the good of the land.

Trials

That the trial of your faith, being much more precious than of gold that perisheth, though it be tried with fire, might be found unto praise and honour and glory at the appearing of Jesus Christ.

1Peter 1:7

The trial of my faith, is much more precious than of gold that perishes, though it be tried with fire, might be found unto praise, honor, and glory at the appearing of Jesus Christ.

Affirmations to
Strengthen Your
Relationship with God
Part 6

❏ I know that by faith God is worthy of all honor, praise and worship as the Creator of all things.

❏ I find inspiration in the Word to do great things.

❏ I will not settle for less than God's best.

❏ I will focus on my achievements and goals and every past failure was a tool God used for my growth and His glory.

❏ I have learned to let go of experiences and I can move forward with God's plan for my life.

❏ I am aware of the words that I speak; therefore, I have girded my mind with the mind of Christ.

❏ I will not be slothful when God calls me.

❏ I am crucified with Christ, nevertheless I live, not I, but Christ lives in me.

❏ I submit myself to God who gives me grace.

❏ Thanks to God, who gives me the victory through my Lord Jesus Christ.

☐ I know that God loves me and chose me in Christ Jesus before the foundation of the world.

☐ As I draw closer to God, He will draw closer to me.

☐ The LORD delights in me because I fear him, and I put my hope in his unfailing love. Psalm 147:11

☐ For God so loved the world that He gave His one and only Son, because I believe in Him I shall not perish but have eternal life. John 3:16

☐ This is my prayer: that my love may abound more and more in knowledge and depth of insight. Philippians 1:9

☐ God is not unjust; He will not forget my work and the love I have shown Him as I have helped His people and I will continue to help them. Hebrews 6:10

☐ I am blessed because I persevere under trial, I have stood the test, and I will receive the crown of life that God has promised to those who love Him. James 1:12

❐ I will obey God's word, so that His love is truly made complete in me. 1 John 2:5

❑ I have a wealth of love to offer the world.

❐ I find inspiration in the things around me.

As I draw closer to God, He will draw closer to me.

HOLINESS

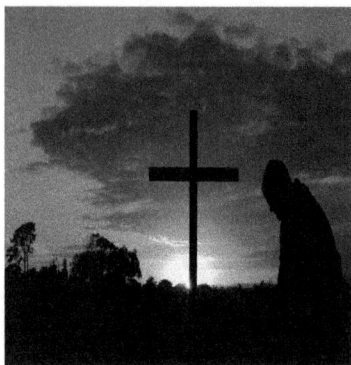

"Be holy, because I am holy."

1 Peter 1:15-16

But just as he who called you is holy, so be holy in all you do; for it is written: "Be holy, because I am holy."

1 Peter 1:15-16

LOVE

His love endures forever. and Og king of Bashan— His love endures forever. and gave their land as an inheritance, His love endures forever. an inheritance to his servant Israel; His love endures forever. to the One who remembered us in our low estate His love endures forever. and freed us from our enemies, His love endures forever. and who gives food to every creature. His love endures forever.

Psalm 136:19-25

For God so loved the world that He gave...

OBEDIENCE

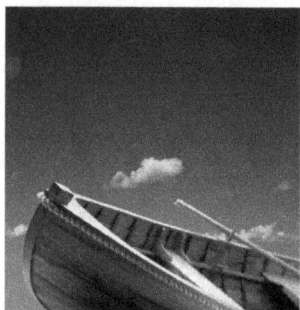

...the way of obedience to the LORD'S commands.

Judges 2:17b

And this is love: that I walk in obedience to his commands. As I have heard from the beginning, his command is that I walk in love.

2 John 1:6

Prayer

Answer me when I call to you, O my righteous God. Give me relief from my distress; be merciful to me and hear my prayer.

Psalm 4:1

Hear my cry, O God; listen to my prayer. From the ends of the earth I call to you, I call as my heart grows faint; lead me to the rock that is higher than I am. You have been my refuge, a strong tower against the enemy.

Psalm 61:1-3

Righteousness

Righteousness goes before him and prepares the way for his steps.

Psalm 85:13

I trust in your unfailing love; my heart rejoices in your salvation. I will sing to You, because You have been good to me.

STRENGTH

The LORD is my strength and my shield; my heart trusts in him, and I am helped. My heart leaps for joy and I will give thanks to him in song.

Psalm 28:7

The LORD is my strength and my shield; my heart trusts in Him.

Worship

All the nations You have made will come and worship before You, O Lord; they will bring glory to Your name.

Psalm 86:9

Worship is God's weapon of choice for my life and I will wield it with precision.

Affirmations of
Confidence
In God
Part 7

☐ The LORD is my light and my salvation—whom shall I fear? The LORD is the stronghold of my life—of whom shall I be afraid? When evil men advance against me to devour my flesh, when my enemies and my foes attack me, they will stumble and fall. Though an army besiege me, my heart will not fear; though war break out against me, even then will I be confident. Psalm 27:1-3

☐ The fruit of my righteousness will be peace; the effect of righteousness will be quietness and confidence forever. Isaiah 32:17

☐ The LORD will be my confidence and will keep my foot from being snared. Proverbs 3:26

☐ I am blessed because I trust in the LORD, my confidence is in Him. Jeremiah 17:7

☐ Such confidence as this is mine through Christ before God. 2 Corinthians 3:4

☐ In this way, love is made complete in my life so that I will have confidence on the day of judgment, because in this world I am like Him. 1 John 4:17

❏ For You have been my hope, O Sovereign LORD, my confidence since my youth. Psalm 71:5

❏ One thing I ask of the LORD, this is what I seek: that I may dwell in the house of the LORD all the days of my life, to gaze upon the beauty of the LORD and to seek Him in His temple. Psalm 27:4

Call on God

I call on You, O God, for You will answer me; give ear to me and hear my prayer.

Psalm 17:6

I call on You, O God, for you will answer me; give ear to me and hear my prayer.

GRACE

She will set a garland of grace on Your head and present You with a crown of splendor."
Proverbs 4:9

God's grace is sufficient for me: for my strength is made perfect in weakness.

Healing

How God anointed Jesus of Nazareth with the Holy Spirit and power, and how He went around doing good and healing all who were under the power of the devil, because God was with Him.

Acts 10:38

When I was down
and in need of
healing, He took
my hand and said,
"Daughter, your
faith has healed
you. Go in peace
because you are
free from your
suffering."

PEACE

I will lie down and sleep in peace, for You alone, O LORD, make me dwell in safety

Psalm 4:8

*When I lie down,
I sleep in peace,
for You alone,
O LORD,
make me reside
in safety and
confident
trust.*

Prosperity

The LORD will grant you abundant prosperity in the fruit of your womb.

Deuteronomy 28:11

The LORD will grant me abundant prosperity in the fruit of my womb.

Trust

Those who know Your name will trust in You, for You, LORD, have never forsaken those who seek You.

Psalm 9:10

I know your name and I will trust in you, for you, LORD, have never forsaken me.

Affirmations of

Peace

Part 8

❐ I will make every effort to live in peace with all men and to be holy; without holiness, no one will see the Lord.

❐ I will strive to live in peace with everybody and pursue consecration and holiness without which no one will ever see the Lord.

❐ I will lie down and sleep in peace, for you alone, O LORD, make me dwell in safety.

❐ Love and faithfulness meet together; righteousness and peace kiss each other and crown my life.

❐ My ways are pleasant ways, and all my paths are peace.

❐ Mercy, peace and love be mine in abundance.

❐ The Lord guides my feet into the path of peace.

❐ The peace of God, which transcends all understanding, guards my hearts and my minds in Christ Jesus.

❐ The Lord's covenant is with me, He has given me a covenant of life and peace.

❏ I am kept by the peace and the power of God.

❏ I am walking in the peace of God that surpasses all understanding.

❏ I will not allow anyone to rob me of my peace.

Affirmations
For
Personal
Growth
Part 9

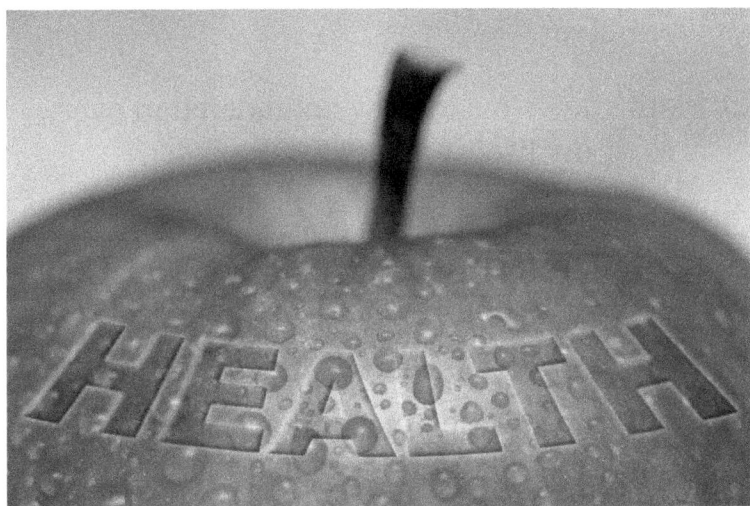

❑ I take personal responsibility for my life and I will not wait for others to validate me.

❑ I will speak life into every situation.

❑ I will catch the vision and make it plain so that I can run with it.

❑ I am a woman that seeks affirmation from God and His word.

❑ I will not allow the things of my past to hinder my destiny.

❑ I am a woman of passion and purpose.

❑ I have the spiritual eyesight to see greatness in others, even when they do not see it in themselves.

❑ Faith allows me to flow unhindered in every area of my life.

❑ The only thing that can hold me back in ME and I will NOT be a hindrance to my destiny.

❑ Destiny awaits my prepared heart.

❑ I will not allow anyone or anything to stand on my feet, therefore I can dance.

My hope is
in You.
My growth
is through
You.

HEALING

But He was pierced for our transgressions, He was crushed for our iniquities; the punishment that brought us peace was upon Him, and by His wounds, we are healed.

Isaiah 53:5

He said to her, "Daughter, your faith has healed you. Go in peace and be freed from your suffering."

Mark 5:34

He was pierced for my transgressions, He was crushed for my iniquities, the punishment that I should have received, He took it for me. By His stripes I am healed.

Knowledge

Teach me knowledge and good judgment, for I believe in Your commands.

Psalm 119:66

Teach me knowledge and good judgment, for I believe in Your commands.

Perfecting

Being confident of this, that He who began a good work in you will carry it on to completion until the day of Christ Jesus.

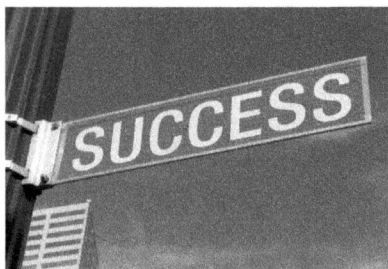

Philippians 1:6

I am convinced and sure of this very thing, that He Who began a good work in me will continue until the day of Jesus Christ right up to the time of His return, developing that good work and perfecting and bringing it to full completion in me.

Prosperity

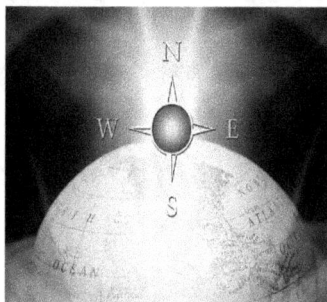

He will spend his days in prosperity, and his descendants will inherit the land.

Psalm 25:13

I am like a tree planted by streams of water, which yields its fruit in season and my leaf does not wither. Whatever I do prospers.

Glory

The heavens declare the glory of God; the skies proclaim the work of His hands.

Psalm 19:1

It does not matter whether I eat or drink or whatever I do, I do it all for the glory of God.

Steps

My steps have held to Your paths; my feet have not slipped.

Psalm 17:5

My steps have held to Your paths; my feet have not slipped. I have learned to walk in Your ways.

Wisdom

My mouth will speak words of wisdom; the utterance from my heart will give understanding.

Psalm 49:3

The mouth of the righteous woman utters wisdom, and my tongue speaks what is just. The law of my God is in my heart; my feet do not slip.

Worship

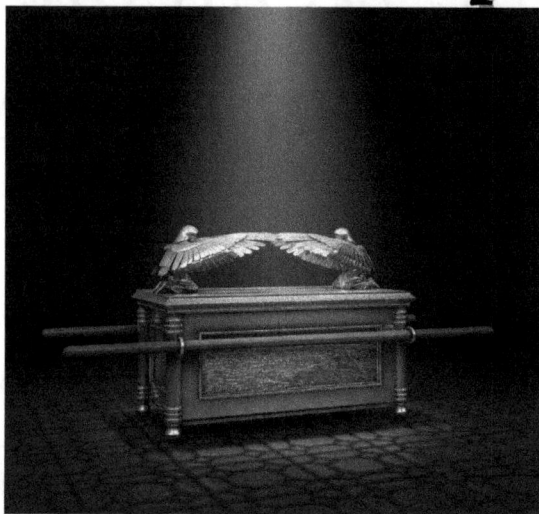

Yet a time is coming and has now come when the true worshipers will worship the Father in spirit and truth, for they are the kind of worshipers the Father seeks.

John 4:23

I will worship the Lord in the beauty of His holiness. I will worship the Lord in spirit and truth.

Affirmations of
Power
Part 10

❏ I am a woman of worth and God's divine power has given me everything I need for life and godliness through my knowledge of Him who called me by His own glory and goodness.

❏ I pray that the eyes of my heart be flooded with light, so that I can understand the hope to which He has called me, and how rich is His glorious inheritance of His set-apart ones, and I can understand what is the immeasurable, unlimited and surpassing greatness of His power in and for me.

❏ I am a woman of worth and I have the God given power within me to be the best I can be and do the best I can do. I am going to wait until I have been clothed with power from on high.

❏ I am Your servant and Your daughter whom You redeemed by Your great power and by Your strong hand.

❏ I exalt you, O LORD, in Your strength; I will sing and praise Your power.

Affirmations
for *Spiritual*
Warfare
Part 11

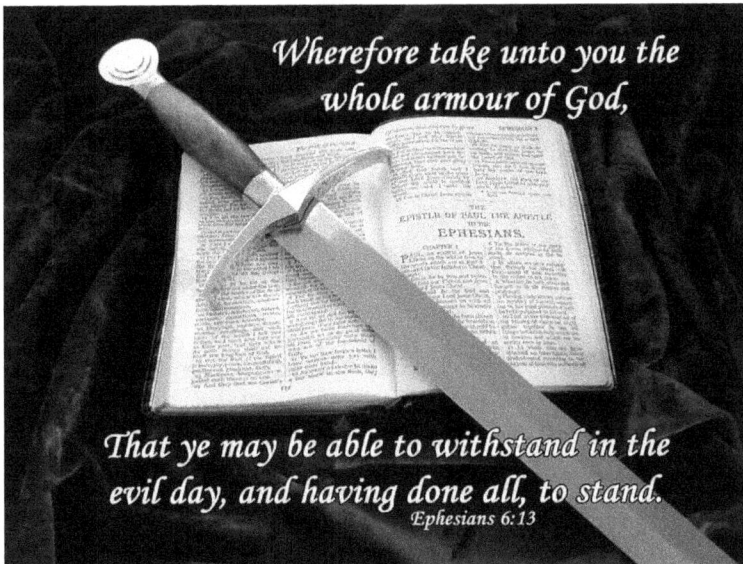

Wherefore take unto you the whole armour of God,

That ye may be able to withstand in the evil day, and having done all, to stand.
Ephesians 6:13

❏ I have put on the full armor of God, so that I will be able to stand firm against the schemes of the devil (Ephesians 6:11).

❏ I have taken up the full armor of God, so that I will be able to resist in the evil day, and having done everything, I will to stand firm (Ephesians 6:13).

❏ Having been justified by faith, I have peace with God through my Lord Jesus Christ, through whom also I have obtained my introduction by faith into this grace in which I stand; and I exult in hope of the glory of God (Romans 5:1-2).

❏ I will be on the alert, stand firm in the faith, and be strong. Let all that I do be done in love (1 Corinthians 16:13-14).

❏ I will put on the full armor of God, so that I will be able to stand firm against the schemes of the devil. My struggle is not against flesh and blood, but against the rulers, against the powers, against the world forces of this darkness, against the spiritual *forces* of wickedness in the heavenly *places*. I will take up the full armor of God, so that I will be able to resist in the evil day, and having done everything, I will stand firm. I will stand firm HAVING GIRDED MY LOINS WITH TRUTH, and HAVING PUT ON THE BREASTPLATE OF RIGHTEOUSNESS, and having shod MY FEET WITH THE PREPARATION OF THE GOSPEL OF PEACE; in addition to all, taking up the shield of faith with which I will be able to extinguish all the flaming arrows of the evil one. I will take THE HELMET OF SALVATION, and the sword of the Spirit, which is the word of God. With all prayer and petition pray at all times in the Spirit, and with this in view, I will be on the alert with all perseverance and petition for all the saints, and pray on my behalf, that utterance may be given to me in the opening of my mouth, to make known with boldness the mystery of the gospel, for which I am an ambassador. (Ephesians 6:11-20).

❑ For I am not ashamed of the gospel, for it is the power of God for salvation to everyone who believes, to the Jew first and also to the Greek (Romans 1:1).

❐ The weapons I fight with are not the weapons of the world. On the contrary, they have divine power to demolish strongholds. I demolish arguments and every pretension that sets itself up against the knowledge of God, and I take captive every thought to make it obedient to Christ (2 Corinthians 10:4-5).

❐ No weapon for against me shall prosper, and every tongue, which rises against me in judgment the Lord shall condemn.

❐ Praises to the God my rock, who trains my hands for war and my fingers for battle against the enemy.

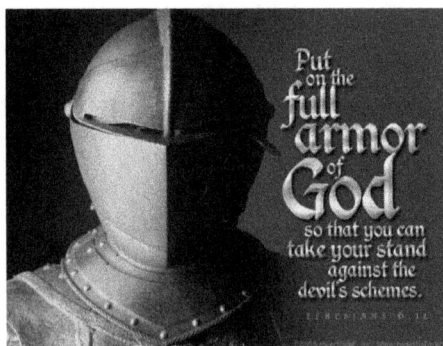

Put on the full armor of God so that you can take your stand against the devil's schemes.

Affirmations
from the
Word of God
Part 12

- ❏ The joy of the Lord is my strength (Nehemiah 8:10).

- ❏ He has made me the head and not the tail (Deuteronomy 28:13).

- ❏ I am are fearfully and wonderfully made (Psalm 139:14).

- ❏ He has prepared a table for me in the presence of my enemies (Psalm 23:5).

- ❏ He has given me peace that surpasses all understanding (Philippians 4:7).

- ❏ He keeps my mind in perfect peace because I keep my mind on Him (Isaiah 26:3).

- ❏ I am an over comer by the Blood of the Lamb and by the words of my testimony (Revelation 12:11).

- ❏ God has brought me out of captivity (Jeremiah 29:14).

- ❏ I am more than a conqueror (Romans 8:37).

- ❏ I have strength for all things in Christ who empowers me (Philippians 4:13 AMP).

☐ The Lord will supply all my needs according to His riches and glory in Christ Jesus (Philippians 4:19).

☐ I can do all things through Christ who strengthens me (Philippians 4:13).

☐ Forgetting those things which are behind me, and reaching forth unto those things which are before me, press toward the mark for the prize of the high calling of God in Christ Jesus (Philippians 3:13-14).

☐ He is able to do exceeding abundantly above all that I ask or think, according to the power that works in me (Ephesians 3:20).

☐ I shall not die, but live, and declare the works of the LORD (Psalm 118:17).

☐ I am not conformed to this world, but I am transformed by the renewing of my mind (Romans 12:2).

☐ I have decided to decree and declare the fullness of God over my life, and it shall be established for me; and the light of God's favor shall shine upon my ways (Job 22:28).

☐ God hath not given me the spirit of fear; but of power, and of love, and of a sound mind (2 Timothy 1:7).

☐ No weapon formed against me will prosper and whatever comes in my direction my God is more than able to destroy it (Isaiah 54:17).

☐ I am steadfast, unmovable, always abounding in the work of the Lord, forasmuch as I know that my labor is not in vain in the Lord (1 Corinthians 15:58).

☐ Out of the abundance of my heart my mouth will speak destiny (Matthew 12:34).

☐ The LORD will give strength to His people; The LORD will bless me with peace. (Psalm 29:11).

☐ The Lord is my Rock, my Fortress, and my Deliverer; my God, my keen and firm Strength in Whom you trust and take refuge, my Shield, and the Horn of my salvation, my High Tower (Psalm 18:2).

☐ I am *"the called"* of Christ for His good purpose (Romans 1:6).

❏ I am a Kingdom woman with a Kingdom assignment and I will not me moved or shaken from His plan for my life.

❏ Talitha cumi, I, __ (Insert your name) __will arise to the destiny that the Lord has me. I will decree the Word of God over every area of my life. I will stand unmovable and unshakeable as I walk into my destiny. I shall not die, but live, and declare the works of the Lord. My life and my destiny are in His hands. He has promised me an expected end that will bring glory to His name. I am a daughter of inheritance and the Lord will perfect that which concerns me. My destiny is sure and every plan that the Lord has for me shall come to pass.

Affirmations of
Strength and Courage From Empowered Women
Part 13

❐ You gain strength, courage, and confidence by every experience in which you really stop to look fear in the face. You are able to say to yourself, "I lived through this horror. I can take the next thing that comes along."

- Eleanor Roosevelt

❐ Live with intention. Walk to the edge. Listen hard. Practice wellness. Play with abandon. Laugh. Choose with no regret. Appreciate your friends. Continue to learn. Do what you love. Live as if this is all there is.

- Mary Anne Radmacher

❐ Joy is what happens to us when we allow ourselves to recognize how good things really are.

- Marianne Williamson

❐ If you don't like something, change it. If you can't change it, change your attitude.

- Maya Angelou

❐ I'm not afraid of storms for I'm learning how to sail my ship.

- Louisa May Alcott

❑ As we light a path for others, we naturally light our own way.

- Mary Anne Radmacher

❑ Whatever your gifting is, it must be cultivated, motivated, stimulated and then activated in order to bring it to it's fullest.

- Dr. Jacquie Hadnot

When you get the choice to sit it out or dance, I hope you dance.
- Lee Ann Womack

Share Your Story and Help Other Women

1. What story of tragedy and triumph would you share with women?

2. How did the tragedy change your life?

3. What did you learn from your trials?

4. How did your trial mold you into the woman you are today?

5. What would you say to women going through a similar trial?

6. Is there anything else you would like women to know?

Mail your testimony:

A Woman of Worth
c/o: Dr. Jacquie Hadnot
It Is Written Ministries
P.O. Box 25894
Overland Park, Kansas 66213

Write out answers to questions and mail along with permission form.

Permission Form

Name:

_____

Address: _____

City\State: _____

Zip Code: _____:

Email Address: _____

Would you like to use your real name? _____

If you prefer not to use your name, choose a pseudo (false name) _____

I, _____
Hereby give Igniting the Fire Publishing and Dr. Jacquelyn Hadnot permission to share my testimony in print such as: Igniting the Fire Magazine, A Woman of Worth: Testimonies from the Threshing Floor and other printed materials used to help women recover from the problems of the past.

_____
_____ (Date)

About the Author

Dr. Jacquelyn Hadnot is an author, teacher and empowerment speaker whose passion is to empower lives through the Word of God.

God has called Dr. Jacquie to encourage, inspire, motivate and activate the gifts of the Spirit in order to raise powerful ministries in the body of Christ. She is becoming a voice on the subject of women's empowerment, prayer, worship and spiritual warfare.

She is recognized as a modern-day apostle with a strong prophetic and psalmist anointing. She has a revelational teaching ministry with a mandate to saturate the world with the Word of God. Jacquie's heart is to see people arise and walk in the destiny and inheritance of the Lord.

She founded It Is Written Ministries in 2002, a publication company, an accounting and consulting firm, and a global radio station. As a retired accountant and financial executive, Jacquie blends ministerial and entrepreneurial applications in her ministry to enrich and empower a diverse audience with skills and abilities to take kingdoms for the Lord Jesus Christ. She is a national and international lecturer, conference speaker, teacher, business trainer, and financial consultant. She also provides consulting services to businesses, churches and individuals.

She has written over thirty books, manuals, and other materials on intimacy with God, prayer, fasting and spiritual warfare. She has also released several music Cds and received numerous music and book publishing awards.

Beyond the pulpit, Jacquie is a talk-show host on both television and radio with her own programs; The Exchange and Light for Your Path, respectively. Weekly, she applies God's wisdom to today's world solutions. Her ministry goal is to make Christ's teachings relevant for today. She also publishes a quarterly magazine.

In addition to her vast experience, Jacquie has a Thd. in Pastoral Theology and a Masters in Ministry Leadership. She is also a wife, mother and grandmother. She and her husband, Minister Gregory Hadnot presently pastor It Is Written Ministries in Kansas City. They also serve as owners and officers of Igniting the Fire Media Group.

A Woman of Worth: The Movement

We are a Kingdom-minded, Kingdom-oriented ministry with a mandate to encourage, empower and motivate women to walk in victory.

A Woman of Worth: Loving the Skin I'm In, hereafter referred to as AWOW is a gathering of women of destiny designed to encourage, inspire and motivate them to reach the destiny and purpose wrapped inside of them. *"For I know the plans I have for you," declares the LORD, "plans to prosper you and not to harm you, plans to give you hope and a future"* (Jeremiah 29:11).

It is time for women to reconnect with the woman God created them to be. For years, many women have been sitting on the back burner, side lined due to low self-esteem, insecurity and inferiority. Many are pregnant with gifts, talents, ministry, peace, joy, healing, praise, dreams, goals and purpose. God has placed "purpose" inside of us.

Our Goal

A Woman of Worth: Loving the Skin I'm In is more than a conference; it is an agent of change in the lives of God's people. Amidst life's labor pains, AWOW's goal is to show women that they have the inner-power to pursue their purpose. It is time to deliver their destiny and birth their dreams. They are often hearing negative and detrimental words that destroy their self-worth. Through the pains of emotional, physical and verbal abuse, many believe the report of the enemy and give up on accomplishing anything in life. Our vision is to empower individuals to reach their full God given potential and release them from the bondage that has held them captive for so many years.

The bible says faith comes by hearing, and hearing by the Word of God. What are they hearing? Often they hear the same record repeating itself. A Woman of Worth is here to change the record and help our sisters hear a new sound. A sound released from heaven that sings, "You are a woman of worth, a treasure beyond price. You are the apple of God's eye and He has great plans for your life."

Services

- To motivate women to realize their purpose and fulfill their God-given assignments.

- To show women how to actualize their dreams through development of business plans, marketing strategies, vision plans and other key elements necessary for birthing their purpose.

- Teach women to maximize their gifts, ideas, talents and potential.

- Distribute food and clothing to families in need year round.

- Provide grants and scholarships to push them into their destiny.

Learn to love your authentic self:

- Move from low self-esteem to unshakable confidence.

- Stay positive and joyful in challenging times.

- Take responsibility for your life.

- Get better results in life by making better decisions.

- Identify priorities and create new choices.

- Take positive action to create change.

- Create a project plan with focus, commitment and motivation.

- Discover the knowledge and power to move life forward.

- Unlock their God given potential.

- Develop leadership skills.

We also provide assistance with other needs:
- Clothing distribution at most conferences.
- Food distribution at the conference.
- Grants or scholarships given at every conference.

A Woman of Worth: *The Series*

A Woman of Worth: The Books

A Woman of Worth is an eight (8) book series that takes you on a journey of discovery, encouragement and empowerment. Through this series, you will travel with Dr. Jacquie Hadnot along the road of devaluation, low self-esteem, domestic violence, healing and deliverance. Once healing and deliverance have taken place, the journey will continue as women discover the purpose and destiny awaiting them in the womb of destiny. As women arise from the pits of pain and despair, they will learn what it means to answer the call and commission of God. They will discover what it means to wear a mantle of authority as they walk into their Kingdom assignment.

Each book in the series takes the reader on a journey that is sure to bring fresh revelation, fresh vision and clarity of purpose. If you have a desire to live a life of passion, purpose and destiny, then this series is for you.

Book #1: *A Woman of Worth: Loving the Skin I'm In* addresses the issues of low self-esteem, devaluation, insecurity and inferiority. Learning to love the skin you are in is not always as easy as we think. In a society where we are judged by our weight, height, skin color, careers or titles, the enemy can bring us to a place where we devalue or look down on ourselves. *Loving the Skin I'm In* takes you on a journey of discovering self-confidence, peace and inner strength. *Also available: A Woman of Worth: Study Guide & Journal*

Book #2: *A Woman of Worth: From Victim to Victor* addresses the issues of domestic violence and its effects on the lives the victors who overcome it. *From Victim to Victor* chronicles the story of a young woman caught up in the cycle of abuse. The book begins with Jayla's story and moves into the realities of today's society where abuse of women is at an all time high. Join Dr. Jacquie as she tells this heart-breaking story with truth and transparency. *Also available: An interactive Study Guide include in the book.*

Book #3: *A Woman of Worth: Dressed to Heal* follows the spiritual, emotional and physical healing of a woman as she answers the call on her life. *Dressed to Heal* takes you on the journey of a woman who is being used to bring healing to the nations. This book outlines the foundation, characteristics and seasons of a woman who is being dressed to heal, to heal a nation. When a woman is healed, she can heal a nation. *Also available: A Woman of Worth: Study Guide & Journal*

Book #4: *A Woman of Worth: Talitha Cumi* encourages women arise to the design and plan that God has for your life. For years, women have been on the backburner of mediocrity due to the issues of life. It is time to ARISE to a new life in Christ because there is an amazing destiny waiting on the other side of adversity, pain and affliction. It is time to arise, come together, lock arms and become the spiritual mothers, mid-wives, sisters and intercessors that are needed in this season. There is purpose, passion and vision waiting to be birthed from the womb of destiny. *Also available: Talitha Cumi! Journal*

Book #5: *Affirmations for a Woman of Worth: I Hope You Dance*, is a collection of prayers, affirmations and declarations for a woman of worth to pray over every area of her life. *Affirmations for a Woman of Worth* is an empowerment tool in a book to help women speak those things that are not as though they were. This book will create an atmosphere for birthing destiny through the power of the spoken word. This book contains over 250 affirmations to make a part of your everyday life as you find joy in dancing the dance of an over comer.

Book #6: *A Woman of Worth: From the Pit to the Promise* chronicles a woman's journey from the pits of poverty, despair, depression and suicide to become a woman of promise, passion and purpose. This book is for women who have been at the depths of despair, hopelessness and helplessness and on the verge of giving up. When a woman does not know the power locked inside, she will wallow in the pit of pity. Discover what it takes to go from the pit to the promise. *Also available: Pit to Promise Journal. (Available: 2014)*

Book #7: *A Woman of Worth: Mantle of Authority* discusses the mantle that God has placed on His women for their Kingdom assignment. We are "the called" in this season, but it is up to us to answer the call. We are given the vision, then the Lord issues the call and once we are prepared, we are given the commission to go forth as Kingdom woman and advance the Kingdom of God. *Mantle of Authority* uncovers the vision, the call and the commission of a woman of worth. (Available: 2015)

Book #8: *A Woman of Worth: Testimonies from the Threshing Floor* shares testimonies from thirty-one (31) women who have walked through the fire, floods and personal tsunamis of life. Each woman shares her testimony candidly as a means to encourage other women to walk in freedom. *Testimonies from the Threshing Floor* will leave you breathless waiting for the next sister to share her story. *Also available: Threshing Floor Journal (Available: 2015)*

Other Books & Materials by Dr. Jacquie

Books in Print
- The Art of Spiritual Warfare (2012) (Book & Journal)
- A Woman of Worth: Loving the Skin I'm In (Book & Journal)
- A Woman of Worth: Loving the Skin I'm In Study Guide
- A Woman of Worth: From Victim to Victor
- A Woman of Worth: Dressed to Heal (Book & Journal)
- Closing the Doors to Satan's Attacks: *Overcoming Fear*
- Trapped in the Arms of Death: *Overcoming Grip of Suicide*
- Your Declaration of Dependence on God
- In the Face of Adversity: *Overcoming Life's Storms*
- The Enemy in Me: *Overcoming Self-Life Issues*
- There's a Famine in the Land: *Overcoming the Great Recession*
- Ignite My Fire, Lord (Book & Journal)
- The Extravagant Love of God: Experiencing the Prophetic Flow
- Cry Aloud, Spare Not! A Prophetic Call to the Fast
- Cry Aloud, Spare Not! The Companion-Study Guide
- Standing for the King: While in the Spotlight of the Media
- Pretty in Pink: Praying Influential Nonsense Free Women
- Unlocking the Power to Get Wealth
- His Mercy Endures Forever: Psalms, Prayers & Meditations
- To Make War with the Saints: Satan's Kingdom Agenda
- A Treasure in the Pleasure of Loving God

➤ Loving God through His Names: 365 Days of the Year

➤ When Fear Crept In

➤ Deeper…

➤ Naked, Broken and Unashamed

➤ Where Is Your God? Have We Lost the Referential Fear of the Lord? (Coming 2014)

Audio Books & Teachings

➤ More of You… (Volume 1)

➤ In the Face of Adversity: Overcoming Life's Storms

➤ Be Not Deceived…

➤ Where Is Your God?

➤ Recognizing Your Due Season

➤ Praying the Healing Scriptures

➤ The Enemy in Me: Overcoming Self-Life Issues

➤ Trusting God in a Season of Discouragement

➤ The Harlot Heart

Music

➤ The Extravagant Love of God

➤ The Spoken Word of Love

➤ His Mercy Endures Forever: Praying the Psalms

DVD

➤ When Your Faith is Being Tested

➤ What Made David Run

- ➢ Agents of Change
- ➢ Virtuous Women of Worship
- ➢ Secrets of the Secret Place (4 volume series 2014)

TO CONTACT DR. JACQUIE:
www.jacquiehadnot.com

Or write us:
jacquie@jacquiehadnot.com
Booking@jacquiehadnot.com

Igniting the Fire Media Group
P.O. Box 25894
Overland Park KS 66213
www.ignitingthefire.net

You can do all things through Christ who strengthens you because you are more than a conqueror and

You can dance!

[1] Affirmations, Remez Sasson

www.ingramcontent.com/pod-product-compliance
Lightning Source LLC
Chambersburg PA
CBHW051824090426
42736CB00011B/1644